NASCAR Truck Series

Gail Blasser Riley
AR B.L.: 3.0
Points: 0.5   MG

The World of NASCAR

NASCAR Truck Series

by Gail Blasser Riley

Reading Consultant:
Barbara J. Fox
Reading Specialist
North Carolina State University

Content Consultant:
Betty L. Carlan
Research Librarian
International Motorsports Hall of Fame
Talladega, Alabama

Capstone press

Mankato, Minnesota

Blazers is published by Capstone Press,
151 Good Counsel Drive, P.O. Box 669, Mankato, Minnesota 56002.
www.capstonepress.com

Library of Congress Cataloging-in-Publication Data
Riley, Gail Blasser.
    NASCAR truck series / by Gail Blasser Riley.
    p. cm. — (Blazers. The World of NASCAR)
    Includes bibliographical references and index.
    ISBN-13: 978-1-4296-1286-9 (hardcover)
    ISBN-10: 1-4296-1286-X (hardcover)
    1. Truck racing — United States — Juvenile literature. 2. NASCAR
Craftsman Truck Series — Juvenile literature. I. Title. II. Series.
GV1034.996.R55 2008
796.7 — dc22   2007029968

Summary: Describes NASCAR's truck series, including the series history,
    truck features, and racetracks.

Essential content terms are **bold** and are defined on the spread where they
first appear.

Editorial Credits
Mandy Robbins, editor; Bobbi J. Wyss, designer; Jo Miller, photo researcher

Photo Credits
AP Images/The Crescent-News/Russ LaBounty, 28; Glenn Smith, 26;
    Terry Renna, 20
Corbis/GT Images/George Tiedemann, 12–13, 16; Reuters/Mark
    Wallheiser, 7
Getty Images for NASCAR/Chris Graythen, cover; Jason Smith, 22–23;
    Getty Images Inc./Allsport/David Taylor, 11; Jamie Squire, 18–19;
    Jonathan Ferrey, 25; Robert Laberge, 5, 6, 8–9; Streeter Lecka, 14

1 2 3 4 5 6 13 12 11 10 09 08

Table of Contents

Starting off with a Bang

February 18, 2000, was a crazy day at Daytona International Speedway. Fans were enjoying the first truck race ever held there.

On lap 57, Kurt Busch's truck tapped
Rob Morgan's. Morgan lost control and
smacked into Geoff Bodine.

Bodine's truck skidded out of control.
It smashed through the **protective fence**
and burst into flames.

protective fence — a tall fence
that separates the fans from the
racing action on the track

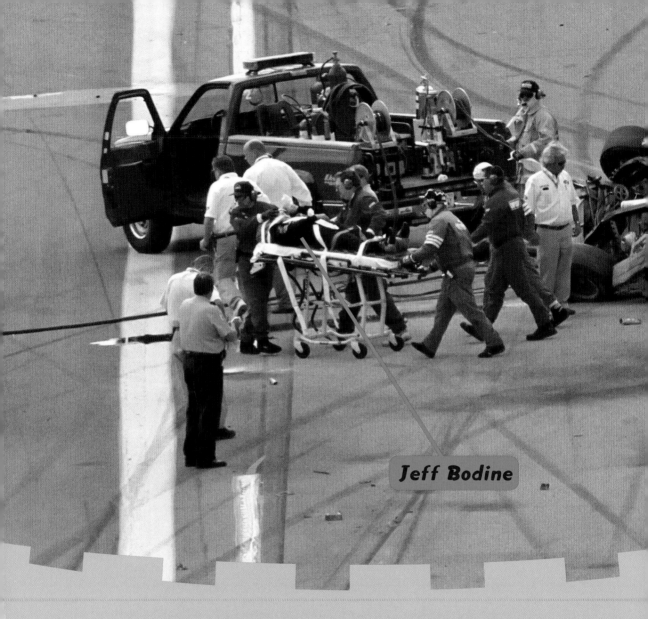

Jeff Bodine

Bodine's truck tumbled down the track. When the dust settled, only the roll cage was left of his truck. Amazingly, Bodine only suffered a few broken bones.

roll cage

TRACK FACT!

Nine fans received minor injuries when Bodine's truck broke through the protective fence.

The Birth of Truck Racing

NASCAR drivers have been racing cars for nearly 60 years. In 1995, they started racing trucks.

2006, John Deere 250

The trucks were harder to handle than cars. This challenge sparked the interest of many drivers. The action-packed races excited fans as well.

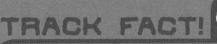

Ted Musgrave

Kyle Busch

14

At first, young stock car drivers raced in the Truck Series. Driving the large trucks improved their skills. Many early truck winners went on to become top Sprint Cup drivers.

TRACK FACT!

Brothers Kurt and Kyle Busch are NASCAR stars who started out in the Truck Series.

2004, Atlanta Motor Speedway

Tough Trucks

NASCAR trucks are built low to the ground to cut *wind resistance*. The closer a truck is to the ground, the faster it can move.

wind resistance — the force of the air that pushes against moving objects

A NASCAR truck does not have doors or side mirrors. Drivers climb in through the windows.

TRACK FACT!

Mike Skinner was the first Truck Series champion. He has raced in the Sprint Cup series too.

Trucks are often taken
to the track in huge haulers.
The haulers carry two trucks,
tools, and equipment.

TRACK FACT!

Some truck haulers have crew
lockers, bunks to nap on, and
an area for watching television.

Truck Diagram

roll cage

front air dam

racing tire

rear wing

racing tire

LUMBER LIQUIDATOR$
1-800-FLOORING
(((XM)))

BOSCH
Team ASE
Snap-on
TRD

23

Tracks for Trucks

The first Truck Series races ran on short tracks. Their **pit roads** weren't large enough for trucks. Races were only 125 miles (201 kilometers) long to cut out pit stops.

pit road — a road that runs off the race track where cars get serviced

Today, trucks race on 2.5-mile
(4-kilometer) speedways like Daytona.
Most tracks now have larger pit roads
to make room for trucks.

Truck races have lots of close finishes and wild crashes. Many fans find them more exciting than car races.

TRACK FACT!

Safety features like roll cages and five-point seatbelts keep drivers safe.

Jack Sprague takes the checkered flag!

The Truck Series has changed a lot since it began in 1995. As the sport continues, fans can expect more exciting racing action.

Glossary

front air dam (FRUNT AIR DAM) — a body panel in the front of a race truck that cuts the wind and makes for a smoother ride

hauler (HALL-uhr) — a special trailer to carry race trucks

pit road (PIT RODE) — a road that runs off the main part of a race track; racers drive down pit road during races for pit stops.

protective fence (pruh-TEK-tiv FENSS) — a safety wall that separates drivers from fans in the stands

rear wing (REER WING) — a wing-shaped part attached to the back of a race truck that helps improve handling

roll cage (ROHL KAYJ) — a structure of strong metal tubing in a race truck that surrounds and protects the driver

wind resistance (WIND ri-ZISS-tuhnss) — the force of the air that pushes against moving objects; wind resistance increases with an object's speed.

Read More

Mattern, Joanne. *Track Trucks.* Stock Car Racing. New York: Children's Press, 2007.

Savage, Jeff. *The World's Fastest Pro Stock Trucks.* Built for Speed. Mankato, Minn.: Capstone Press, 2003.

Woods, Bob. *Earning a Ride: How to Become a NASCAR Driver.* The World of NASCAR. Chanhassen, Minn.: Child's World, 2004.

Internet Sites

FactHound offers a safe, fun way to find Internet sites related to this book. All of the sites on FactHound have been researched by our staff.

Here's how:
1. Visit *www.facthound.com*
2. Choose your grade level.
3. Type in this book ID **142961286X** for age-appropriate sites. You may also browse subjects by clicking on letters, or by clicking on pictures and words.
4. Click on the **Fetch It** button.

FactHound will fetch the best sites for you!

Index